MAKING
SOAPS

To Filippo

Thanks to Maurizio Minora, Chiara Gelmetti, Anna Giulietti, Marina Tognolo, Nicoletta Romanelli, Thea Zuliani, my mother.
To LUSH, via Fiori Chiari 6, Milan, Italy.
Special thanks to Monique Chauliac and Daniel Lalauze, Fabrication de Savons, 13 Grand'rue, 07200 Aubenas, France.

Author's e-mail address: paolarom@katamail.com

Soapmaking Suppliers

Sun Feather Natural Soap Company
1551 State Route 72
Potsdam, NY 13676
Tel: 800-771-7627
Lye, fats, soap fragrance, soap color, essential and fragrance oils, molds, equipment, dried botanicals, and soap bases.

Bramble Berry Soapmaking Supplies
1208 Bay Street, Suite C
Bellingham, WA 98225
Tel: 360-734-8278
Fax: 360-752-0992
Web site: http://www.brambleberry.com/
Vegetable oils, preservatives, essential and fragrance oils, containers, glycerin, citric acid, molds, melt-and-pour supplies.

Rainbow Meadow, Inc.
P.O. Box 457
Napoleon, MI 49261
Tel: 517-817-0021
Toll Free (U.S. & Canada): 1-800-207-4047
Fax: 800-219-0213
Web site: http://www.rainbowmeadow.com/
Vegetable and essential oils, glycerin, citric acid, dyes, soap molds, melt-and-pour supplies, pigments, clays, sodium & potassium hydroxide, gel colorants

Editorial direction: Cristina Sperandeo
Photography: Alberto Bertoldi
Graphic design and layout: Paola Masera and Amelia Verga
Cover: Damiano Viscardi
Translation: Studio Queens

Originally published in Italy © 1999 RCS Libri S.p.A., Milan, Italy
under the title *Saponi e saponette*
Distributed in 2002 to the trade and art markets in North America by
North Light Books,
an imprint of F&W Publications, Inc.
4700 East Galbraith Road
Cincinnati, OH 45236
(800) 289-0963

Printed in Italy

ISBN 1-58180-328-1

Metric Conversion Chart

To convert	to	multiply by
Inches	Centimeters	2.54
Centimeters	Inches	0.4
Feet	Centimeters	30.5
Centimeters	Feet	0.03
Yards	Meters	0.9
Meters	Yards	1.1
Sq. Inches	Sq. Centimeters	6.45
Sq. Centimeters	Sq. Inches	0.16
Sq. Feet	Sq. Meters	0.09
Sq. Meters	Sq. Feet	10.8
Sq. Yards	Sq. Meters	0.8
Sq. Meters	Sq. Yards	1.2
Pounds	Kilograms	0.45
Kilograms	Pounds	2.2
Ounces	Grams	28.4
Grams	Ounces	0.04

Paola Romanelli

MAKING SOAPS

NORTH LIGHT BOOKS
Cincinnati, Ohio

CONTENTS

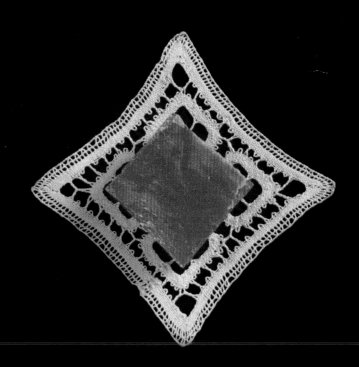

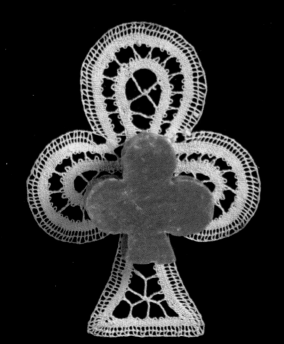
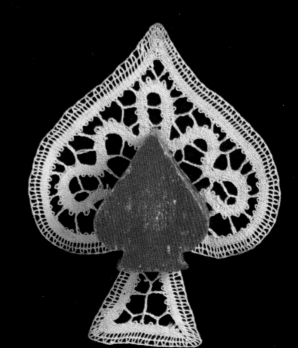

INTRODUCTION

This book is dedicated to your body. If you want to take care of yourself, enhance and improve your image using natural products, you will surely enjoy the craft of soap-making.

I will teach you to make bars of soap enriched with special ingredients to rejuvenate, moisturize, soften or tone your skin, as well as reactivate your blood circulation and find relief from the day's stress.

To get soapmaking down to a fine art, it is essential to spend time. Carefully select all ingredients to make sure they are pure, authentic, and of top quality. When selecting fragrances, be sure to use essential oils of known origins.

With a bit of help from a qualified herbalist or a good book on herbs, you only need to follow my instructions once, and you will have learned the art and techniques of soapmaking. You will soon be able to create your own recipes.

You will love the way the handmade soap feels on your skin and feel confident that it is pure and of top quality.

There are endless combinations of colors, fragrances and shapes to make your own unique bar of soap.

HISTORY

Thousands of years before Christ, the first substances to be used as cleansers were talcum, clay, and ash. Ancient books mention a kind of soap made by mixing soapbark ash with greasy substances, and a special type of soap, added with colorings, which were used by women both to cleanse their hair and to give it extra shine and a richer color.

In the eighteenth century, soap was made in Italy and Spain, and later in France, where it was industrially produced in Marseille. It was mostly made from goat tallow mixed with beech-tree ash.

By the end of the eighteenth century, olive oil soap was introduced and eventually with the addition of lead oxide, glycerine was produced.

This discovery stimulated research on the nature of fats and oils and, in 1823, the chemical reaction that produces fatty acids and glycerine was finally defined through the breakdown of simple fatty acids and their combination with alkali. This chemical reaction is called saponification.

It was our grandmothers' utter delight to unwrap the precious boxes of exquisitely fine soap offered as a tribute to their beauty. At the beginning of the twentieth century, all major perfume manufacturers started competing to launch the finest-scented bars of soap on the cosmetics market.

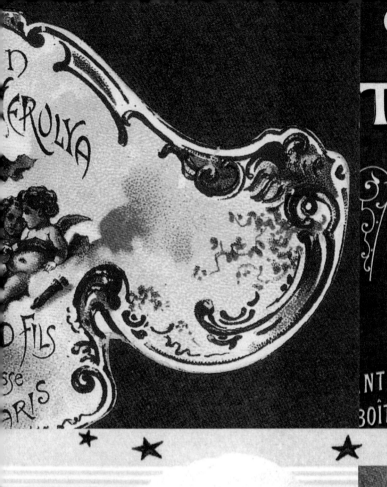

SAVON
DE LA
TULIPE

LESSIVE
DE LA COMÈTE

SAVONNERIE DE LA
COMÈTE
PARIS - St DENIS

SOAP

From a chemical point of view, soap is a salt: it is obtained from a process called saponification, that is, a reaction of fatty acids or oils with a base (sodium hydroxide). Such reaction brings out the salt from the fatty acid – that is, soap – plus glycerine. The molecule of soap resembles a chain with a hydrophile (water-friendly) head, attracted by water, and a lipophile (fat-friendly) tail, attracted by insoluble oils. Soap is therefore a cleanser, because it has the property of emulsifying fats and oils. Emulsion makes otherwise insoluble substances water-soluble. Soap also strongly reduces the surface tension of water. Thus, soapy water clings to the skin better than water alone can do.

HOW TO MAKE IT

If you make soap at home, you must be especially careful when handling alkaline solutions (sodium hydroxide), also known as lye. Since lye is corrosive, remember to wear gloves and to take off all jewelry before working with it.

To make soap with animal fats, you need about 3kg (just over 6lbs) of fat taken from the area of the ox's or pig's kidneys, or pork's lard which you should be able to buy from your butcher. Chop the fat into small chunks and place them in a large pot. Cover with water and add 4 tablespoons of salt; place on the cooking-stove, and every so often stir with a wooden spoon. When all the fat has melted, drain it with a strainer and put it to rest in the refrigerator.

Let it cool overnight and it will turn into a solid, white-colored and compact substance (tallow). Since the fat-refining process often produces unpleasant smells, you may prefer to use ready-made tallow.

Slowly add 350g (12.3oz) of lye to 1.2l (1.2qt.) of cold water and gently stir with a wooden spoon. Heat up a stainless steel pot with 2.7kg (a little less than 6lbs.) of tallow till this melts completely. Cool down to 30°C (86°F) and slowly pour in the lye water, which must have already been brought to the temperature of 24°C (75.2°F), stirring gently. Stir until the mixture has a honey-like consistency. While the soap is hot, pour it into a wooden mold or a cardboard box lined with wet cloth and covered with linen, so as to avoid dispersion of heat. Let it cool for 48 hours. Wearing gloves, remove the soap from the mold; do not touch it with your bare hands, for it will still be caustic. Warm up the blade of a sharp knife in boiling hot water and cut the soap into bars. Let the bars rest on a screen or sieve for two weeks in an airy, dry place.

The same procedure applies to vegetable soap, in which animal fat is replaced by a mixture of vegetable oils chosen among castor, coconut, soy, avocado, palm, hazelnut, olive oil and others, plus 200g (7oz) of cocoa butter and about 700g (1lb, 9oz) of pectin, a vegetable thickening additive.

Keep in mind that vegetable soap takes its shape and dries slower than animal fat soap, and it should not be heated at high temperatures. Even when making animal fat soap, always add some vegetable oil (coconut, palm, olive, soy, or corn oil), which will improve the soap's qualities, ensuring a longer lasting lather and better cleansing power, and making the soap softer.

These soaps, made by Lush, recall the ancient art of soapmaking. With an all vegetable base, all natural, fresh ingredients, and essences and colorings not tested on animals, these cakes of soap are produced in large shapes to be sliced with a knife.

MINCED SOAPS

The expression "minced soap" stands for soap that is cut into small pieces, or even grated, mixed with water, then melted in a bain-marie (double boiler) and cooled.

The advantage of minced soaps is that they usually have a milder mix and last longer. You can add any ingredient of your liking, such as fragrances and colorings. Now have fun giving different shapes to your soap!

TOOLS

– A cheese grater with different-size holes to mince the soap. With a softer soap base, a wider-hole shredder is recommended.
– A food digital scale to accurately weigh the amount of minced soap and water to be added.
– A double boiler for melting the minced soap. The pot for the soap should be steel, enamel or glass; do not use pots of any other material.
– A water measuring cup.
– A wooden spoon to stir the melting soap.
– A thermometer scaled up to 100°C (212°F) to check the melting soap temperature, which should not be over 65-70°C (149-158°F).
– A food processor to mince the additives for the soap base (indispensable for making floating bars of soap).
– A sieve (ideal for drying bars of soap).

THE BASICS

The raw material for making bars of soap is... soap. Choose your favorite kind of soap, whether made from animal fat or vegetable oils, and mince it with a shredder. Store unused shredded soap in a box that can be sealed, so you can use it on later occasions. Marseille soap is ideal for this purpose: it comes in large, soft pieces and has no additives such as colorings or scents.
You can also buy pre-minced soap, which comes in small white fragments, ready for use.

Also soap flakes can be handy, as they spare you the shredding process. If you like to recycle bits of used soap, store them in a glass jar and, once you have collected enough, melt them: you will have a ready base for new multi-colored bars.

Glycerine is usually sold in 350g (12.4oz) blocks; it is clear and transparent. It is best to break it in fragments before melting in a double boiler (there is no need to add water).

ADDITIVES

Any soap base can be enriched with additives to enhance its properties, to change the way it looks, its scent and also to make it last longer. To make soap with fresh ingredients, you can use fruit and vegetables in season: simply wash them, peel them, and mix. Certain vegetables and fruits, such as carrots or kiwis, give the soap their delicate colors, so you won't need to add any other coloring. Fresh ingredients are often flavored with benzoin, an aromatic, balsamic resin known for its properties as a perfume preservative and fixative. Benzoin is extracted from tapping the bark of spicewood. Benzoin gum is sold in selected herbalist's shops or health food store and comes in small chunks or in powder. Aromatic and medicinal herbs finely chopped, fresh or dried, keep their original properties when added to soap. Use mallow (hibiscus) or calendula (marigold petals). Milk, honey, oils and cocoa butter are commonly added to soap for their skin softening properties. Whenever milk is added, we recommend the use of powdered milk.

Body-scrubbing soap is made by adding grain flour or husk. These additives are somewhat rough and help to exfoliate dead skin layers. You may also add very fine sand, once washed and cleared of any impurities. Please note: scrubbing soap is *not* suitable as face soap!

Spices such as cinnamon, ginger, saffron, cloves, and nutmeg are easy to find and give soap their marvellous spicy scents. Crumbled or ground into your soap, they will add an oriental touch to your cleansing routine.

COLORINGS

Although most bars of soap are tinted to look more attractive, it is not necessary to color soap. Still, coloring can make it easier to distinguish between soaps with different ingredients. Baby soap is generally plain and uncolored since it is not supposed to contain additives such as colorings or perfumes.

Good-quality colored soap should produce a white lather: soap that makes colored lather should be avoided since it will stain your skin and clothes. The coloring should be added with a medicine dropper

when the soap is still in its melting state and should be blended in very well, making certain that it dyes the mixture evenly.

Traditional colorings for soap are the same as those used to dye wax: they come in wax disks, to be melted in vegetable oil on a low fire and are added to the mixture before it is poured into the molds.

Fabric colorings, either liquid or powdered, also give good results. They should be used in very small amounts because of their high dyeing power: you can always add more should the color look too weak. Fabric colorings contain sodium, so bear in mind that large amounts may damage your soap. Powdered colorings should be melted in hot water first and then blended into the soap mixture before pouring it into the mold.

Food colorings are often used to dye soap, though they should also be used with moderation. It is enough to add a few drops to the mixture with a dropper. Be aware that food colorings tend to fade with time.

Mineral pigments are extracted from rocks and can be found in paint shops, since they are commonly used for painting. They are powdered and must always be melted in water first and added to the mixture only at the end of the process.

Vegetables and fruit color soap with their pleasant, delicate hues, which you may like to strengthen with a drop coloring. The addition of oils, butter and honey gives soap an amber color as well as softness.

Spices, in particular, give strong colors to soaps: powdered cinnamon, cloves, and nutmeg allow for colors with all shades of brown; saffron, turmeric, and curry make it yellow to orange; cayenne pepper and paprika usually give soap a salmon color. Once powdered, these spices must be added directly to the mixture: 1-2 teaspoons per 350g (12.4oz) of soap. Any excess will produce soap with a very "spicy" lather. Decoctions and teas made with dyeing herbs must be left to decant six to eight hours and must be kept in the refrigerator prior to being blended into melted soap.

SCENTS

Washing with scented soap creates more than just a short moment of pleasure, for your skin will absorb and keep its scent for quite some time. Accordingly, aside from the use of a good soap, before you add scents, make sure you are not allergic to them.

You can easily do this by testing a small area on your body, such as the inner part of your wrist.

Soap is generally scented with "essential oils". The terms "essential oils" and "scented essences" refer to extremely volatile, very strongly scented natural substances of vegetable or animal origin.

Vegetable essences contained in the leaves, flowers, or in the whole plant have very different scents from each other. They are usually extracted by distillation through a steam flow.

Essential oils are not only used by the perfume and cosmetics industries, but also in the pharmaceutical sector.

Scented essences will also provide therapeutic properties. For instance, soap with essential mallow oil has a soothing effect on your skin and will soften and protect it from environmental damage.

A few drops are generally enough to scent a bar of soap: add essential oils sparingly because they are so potent.

Since natural essential oils are expensive (because of both the high cost of raw materials and the complexity of the extraction procedure), today many are produced industrially by a process of chemical synthesis. These synthetic oils do not have therapeutic properties and, accordingly, cannot be used in natural practices, such as aromatherapy. Cheap synthetic oils especially should not be used, for they are diluted and, therefore, do not scent the soap strongly enough. Alcohol-based oils should also be avoided.

Remember that all scents tend to fade away with time, no matter what type of oil they are mixed with. In order to prevent them from losing their scent too quickly, you can add a fixative, such as benzoin, during the soapmaking process.

MOLDS

The shape of soap is obviously created by its mold. For large bars of soap, the molds commonly available often reproduce geometrical shapes such as cubes, or large cylinders. For smaller bars of soap (especially the glycerin-based ones), there is a wider choice of molds in the shapes of animals, shells, angels, hearts, etc. Molds are made of heat-resistant plastic, which can stand the high temperature of melted soap. They are also flexible so that the bars of soap can be removed easily, just by gently pressing the bottom of the mold, without spoiling their shapes. The bottom of the mold

is usually smaller than the upper part, and the walls are slanted so that the soap can slip out easily when the mold is turned upside down. Some molds are engraved with ornaments, logos, brand names and so on, so that their decorations can be impressed on the soap. You can also use molds not especially designed for soapmaking, such as candle or plaster casts, as long as they present all the characteristics mentioned above. Besides, a good look around your kitchen will give you plenty of ideas: experiment with using cookie cutters, ice-cream cups, or any other suitable food container! You could also use a PVC pipe, or any plastic cylinder, and then slice the soap to make disks. Large molds such as baking pans, trays, or flowerpot holders allow you to cut your soap into smaller shapes of your liking. If you feel that a mold has a difficult shape to extract your soap from, just spray the mold with a vegetable cooking spray before you pour the soap mixture into it. Also, to extract the soap from the mold with ease, leave the mold in the freezer for a few hours after the soap has been poured into it.

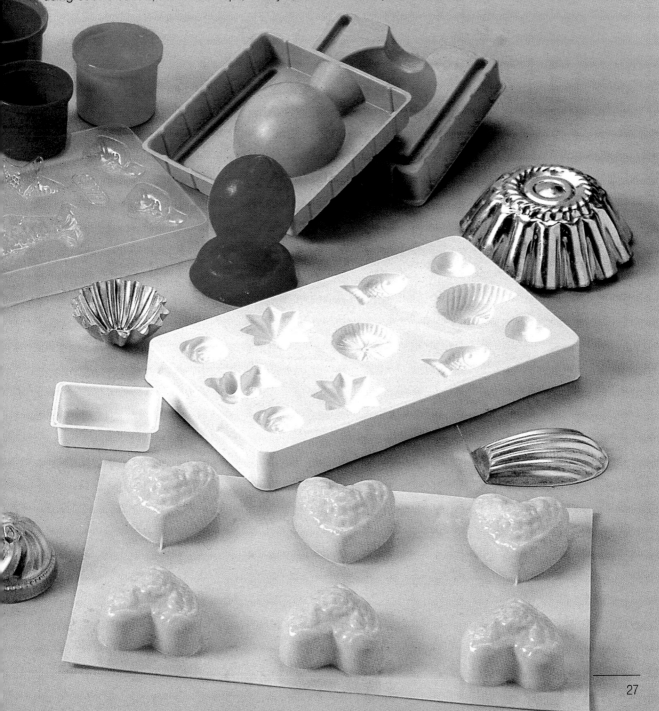

THE PH VALUE

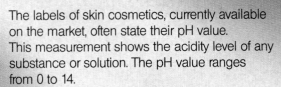

The labels of skin cosmetics, currently available on the market, often state their pH value. This measurement shows the acidity level of any substance or solution. The pH value ranges from 0 to 14.
A pH of 7 indicates a neutral solution; if the pH is less than 7, the solution is acidic, whereas a pH of more than 7 indicates an alkaline (or base) solution.

The pH value can be tested with litmus paper. Litmus paper has the property of changing its color. It will turn red in an acidic solution and blue in an alkaline one. PH values between 5.5 and 10.5 are skin- and hair-friendly, even though this value is usually limited to a range between 5.5 and 8.0.

SOAPMAKING TECHNIQUE

In spite of the huge number of cosmetics available nowadays, nothing will replace the pleasure of taking a delicately-scented, exquisitely-shaped bar of fine soap out of its precious gift wrap. Making one's own soap is becoming more and more popular for its benefits. It is not only exciting to create a cosmetic that appeals to your personal taste, but also it is reassuring, as it guarantees the quality of your formula and allows you to add natural ingredients to answer all your skin's specific "cries for help". But soapmaking requires you to master its techniques, which are what you'll learn in the following pages.

SIMPLE SOAPS

All minced soaps, mentioned
in the following recipes,
should be made with 120g (4.2oz)
of shredded soap and 90g (3.2oz) of
water. The amount of mixture you get will be
enough for three medium-size bars. You may vary the
quantities, but you must keep to this ratio. Any excess water,
as an additive, will cause your soap to shrink during the
drying process, thus altering its shape and surface.

- soap
- cheese grater
- double boiler
- wooden spoon
- thermometer
- molds of your
  choice
- bottle of coloring
  with dropper
- fragrance
- non-serrated knife
- sieve
- digital scales
- liquid measuring
  cup
- mesh screen

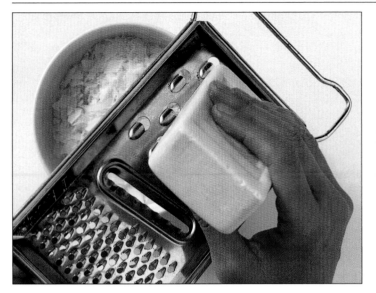

1 – Cover your work table with newspaper and shred a large piece of soap.

2 – Weigh 120g (4.2oz) of soap flakes.

3 – Pour into a double boiler.

4 – Add water a little at a time, stirring with a wooden spoon, every so often, until the soap flakes melt in the water and make an even mixture.

5 – Once you have a smooth mixture, take its temperature, which should not exceed 65–70°C (149–158°F).

6 – Now put in the additives. Add a few drops of your chosen coloring and stir gently so the color blends well.

7 – If you're using powdered coloring, dilute it in a little warm water first and then add it to the mixture with a medicine dropper.

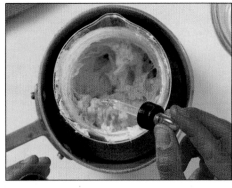

8 – Stir your mixture well.

9 – Choose your favorite fragrances and add three to four drops (at most) with a medicine dropper. If you're using essential oils, stick to the amount suggested on the label. The amount for both colorings and scents is very much up to you, but be careful not to overdo it either. With a little experience you will be able to get exactly the color hues and intensity of fragrance you wish.

10 – When fragrance and colorings are uniform in the soap mixture, let the soap cool.

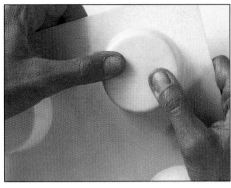

11 – Make sure your molds are perfectly clean, spray with vegetable oil and fill them using a wooden spoon. Beat the mold on the table every now and then in order to get rid of any air bubbles that may have formed inside.

12 – Smooth the outside surface with a knife and let it cool off. When it is lukewarm, put it in the freezer for about two hours to make extracting it easier. Turn the mold upside down, push gently on the bottom and knock it on the table.

13 – The soap will still be soft when it comes out of the mold, so handle it with care. Place it on a mesh screen to dry. If its shape looks irregular, you can smooth it out with a knife.

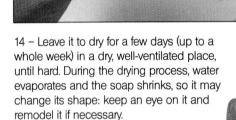

14 – Leave it to dry for a few days (up to a whole week) in a dry, well-ventilated place, until hard. During the drying process, water evaporates and the soap shrinks, so it may change its shape: keep an eye on it and remodel it if necessary.

To clean the soap off all your tools, including the molds, soak them in lukewarm water for an hour, after which time the soap will come off easily under running water.

SPECIAL
RECIPES

COFFEE SOAP

Keep this soap in your kitchen, nice and handy, because its ingredients are great for getting rid of unpleasant odors such as fish, onion, and garlic.

- 120g (4.2oz) of shredded soap
- 90g (3.2oz) of water
- 1 tbsp. (15g, 0.5oz) of freshly-ground coffee
- $^1/_2$ tsp. of powdered benzoin a pinch of cardamom
- cheese grater

8
C
th
s

SULPHUR SOAP
(Anti-bacterial)

Due to its sulphur content, this soap has a strong cleansing action and anti-bacterial power. It is suitable for oily skins as well as preventing and treating bacterial infections.

- 120g (4.2oz) of soap flakes
- 90g (3.2oz) of water
- $^{1}/_{2}$ tsp. of sulphur powder
- a few drops of tea tree essence

Sulphur gives this soap a pleasant, bright yellow color. Gently mix a few grams ($^{1}/_{10}$oz) of sulphur powder with the soap (sulphur powder can be found in herbalist's shops). Finally, add a few drops of tea tree essence to curb the acrid smell of sulphur.

SEAWEED SOAP

Dried seaweed used in food recipes makes a great ingredient for soap, because it contains iodine and vitamins. Seaweed also has a strong dyeing power on soap.

- 120g (4.2oz) of soap flakes
- 90g (3.2oz) of water
- 5-10g (0.2-0.4oz) of seaweed
- essential oil of your choice

Add dried or powdered seaweed, such as focus, when the soap is still melting. Seaweed has a peculiar smell, and you may want to scent your soap with a few drops of fragrance oil.

POLLEN SOAP

This soap has a nourishing effect on your complexion, though it is not recommended for sensitive skin. Add the millefiori pollen to the melting soap and blend the pollen with the mixture. Add a few drops of flower essence, which will leave a lovely scent on your skin. If you like, you can add some yellow, ochre or orange coloring.

- 120g (4.2oz) of soap flakes
- 90g (3.2oz) of water
- 5-10g (0.2-0.4oz) of millefiori pollen
- a few drops of flower essence
- colorings: yellow, ochre, orange

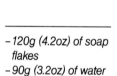

EXOTIC ESSENCE SOAP

With its intense, marvelous aromas, soap with exotic essences recalls an oriental atmosphere. The essential oil extracted from sandalwood, for instance, gives soap a moisturizing and balancing power over dry skin.

- *120g (4.2oz) of soap flakes*
- *90g (3.2oz) of water*
- *colorings: all shades of brown*
- *essential oils of aromatic woods of your choice (sandalwood, cedar, tea tree)*

 Add the oils to the melting soap and color the mixture with different pigments.

CLAY SOAP

Adding clay (a fine powder in various colors: green, gray, brown or reddish) to soap produces an excellent cleanser for oily skin, and is also very good for calming skin rashes. Mix a teaspoon of clay with the melting soap, stirring constantly until the mixture is soft. There is no need to add coloring, since clay is itself a powerful dye.

–120g (4.2oz) of soap
  flakes
– 90g (3.2oz) of water
– 1 tsp. of clay

FRUIT AND VEGETABLE SOAP

The following section will teach you how to make fruit and vegetable soaps. The all-natural composition of these soaps is especially formulated to help you keep your skin balanced, moisturized and revitalized while also keeping you clean.

KIWI FRUIT SOAP

Rich in vitamins, minerals and proteins, kiwi is available in the produce section of your local supermarket.

- 120g (4.2oz) of vegetable soap flakes
- 1 kiwi fruit
- 110g (3.8oz) of water
- 1 tsp. of benzoin
- ylang-ylang essential oil
- green coloring

Peel, slice, and mix a kiwi fruit to create a kiwi pulp. Add up to 110g (3.8oz) of water. Add in the soap and melt the mixture in a double boiler. Finally, add a teaspoon of benzoin and a few drops of ylang-ylang. You may like to brighten the color of your soap by adding a little green coloring.

CARROT SOAP

Carrots are among the vegetables with the highest vitamin content: besides carotene (which produces vitamin A), they are rich in vitamin B1 and vitamin C. The presence of such vitamins makes carrot soap extremely healthy for your skin.

- 120g (4.2oz) of vegetable soap flakes
- 90g (3.2oz) of water
- 1 carrot
- 1 tsp. of benzoin

Vitamins are concentrated in the outer part of the carrot root, which is why this vegetable should never be peeled or scraped.

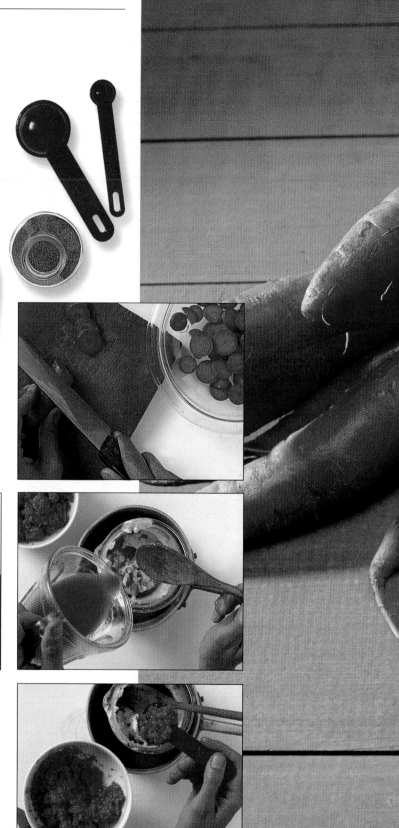

Slice the carrot and mix it in a little water. Drain it with a strainer and set aside the pulp.
Gently add the water to the carrot juice and melt the soap in the mixture.
Gently stir in a tablespoon of carrot pulp, which will immediately give the mixture its delicate orange color. Add a teaspoon of benzoin. Pour the mixture into the mold, let it dry completely, and get ready to wash yourself with a bar of soap packed with healthy vitamins!

LEMON SOAP

Not only does this lemon soap look like the real thing, but also it contains disinfectant properties and is very effective in re-balancing oily skin and revitalizing a dull complexion.

- 120g (4.2oz) of vegetable soap flakes
- 90g (3.2oz) of water
- 2 lemons
- $1/2$ tsp. of benzoin
- lemon essence

Squeeze one lemon and gently add its juice to the water. Wash the second lemon and grate its rind (it is important to add the rind because of its high vitamin C content).

Melt the soap flakes in water and lemon juice. Add in the grated lemon rind, benzoin and a few drops of lemon essence, and stir. Grease a lemon-shaped, rubber candle mold with a little olive oil, and pour the mixture into the mold.

COCONUT SOAP

Because of the addition of coconut oil, this soap is particularly suitable for dry, rough and wrinkled skin.

Combine the soap flakes with water. Melt the mixture in a double boiler, add ground coconut pulp and gently stir so it blends in well. When you have made a uniform mixture, add the benzoin and coconut oil.

– 120g (4.2oz) of vegetable soap flakes
– 90g (3.2oz) of water
– 15g (0.5oz) of ground coconut pulp
– 1 tsp. of benzoin
– 1 tsp. of coconut oil

CUCUMBER SOAP

Cucumber is particularly suitable for your skin because it cleanses and moisturizes at the same time. This soap is therefore recommended for everyday use as a face cleanser.

- 120g (4.2oz) of vegetable soap flakes
- water
- 1 small green cucumber
- 1 tsp. of benzoin
- green coloring

Wash well, slice and mix a small cucumber. Weigh the mixture and add water up to 110g (3.8oz). Melt the soap in the cucumber pulp. Add benzoin and stir: Your soap will immediately take on a green color. If you wish to make it look even brighter, add some green coloring.

MEDICINAL HERB SOAP

Sage, rosemary, althaea, lavender, and many more herbs have healing properties that you can add to homemade soap. Some moisturize, others soften and soothe, your skin. Every bar of soap takes on the color and scent of the plant it contains. For a brighter tone, it is best to add coloring chosen in the same color as the part of the plant you have used.

MALLOW SOAP

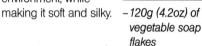

Mallow, a common plant
in grassy areas, has lovely
pale pinkish, purple blossoms. It soothes skin
irritations, helps to remove impurities and
protects your skin from the harsh effects of the
environment, while
making it soft and silky.

- 120g (4.2oz) of
  vegetable soap
  flakes
- 90g (3.2oz) of water
  for the infusion
- 10g (0.4oz) of dried
  mallow blossoms
- 1 tbsp. of honey
- rose essence
- purple coloring

Prepare a mallow infusion.
Melt the soap in a double boiler with the
mallow infusion, stirring constantly until you
get an even mixture. Add the dried mallow
blossom petals. Blend in a tablespoon of
honey to enhance the softening properties of
mallow and add a small amount of diluted
delicate purple coloring powder. Dilute the
powder beforehand in warm water.

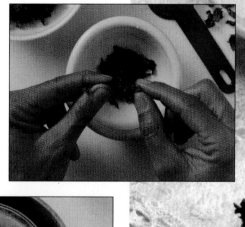

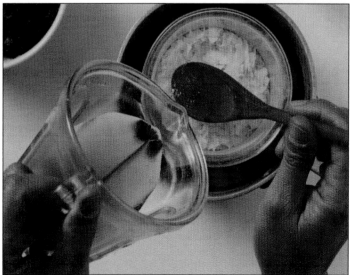

CALENDULA SOAP

Calendula (marigold) softens your skin and makes it more supple. The plant's healing properties are concentrated in the blossoms, and can be added either dried or fresh to the soap mixture.

- 120g (4.2oz) of vegetable soap flakes
- 90g (3.2oz) of water
- 10g (0.4oz) of dried calendula blossoms
- calendula oil

Gently remove the colored petals from the dried calendula blossoms. Melt the soap with the water in a double boiler. Add the petals, stirring gently. Add one to two drops of calendula oil before pouring the soap into the molds.

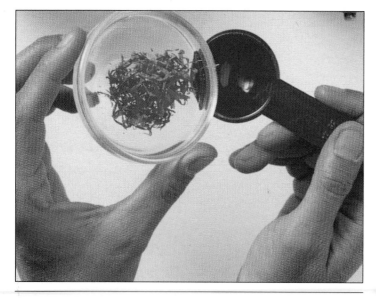

SAGE SOAP

Sage has refreshing properties that are very useful whenever excess perspiration may be a problem. There are also sage shampoos that stimulate your hair's growth.

– 120g (4.2oz) of vegetable soap flakes
– 90g (3.2oz) of water
– 10g (0.4oz) of dried sage leaves
– sage essential oil
– green coloring

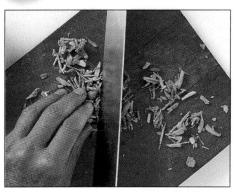

Finely chop the dried sage leaves. Add them to the soap while it is melting in a double boiler. Add a few drops of sage fragrance oil to enhance the scent of sage, and add a little green coloring.

CHAMOMILE SOAP

This soap is particularly suitable for delicate skin as it has good soothing properties. If used as an ingredient in shampoo, chamomile makes your hair softer and blonder. However, chamomile cosmetics are not recommended for anyone suffering from skin allergies.

- 120g (4.2oz) of vegetable soap flakes
- 90g (3.2oz) of water
- 10g (0.4oz) of chamomile blossoms or one sachet of chamomile
- lemon essence
- yellow coloring

As dried chamomile blossoms tend to leave dark stains on soap, it is best to give the mixture a strong color if you want your soap to look well. Chamomile in sachets is easier to blend in with the mixture.

Make a chamomile tea and steep at least 15 minutes. Add tea and soap in the double boiler; then add to the soap mixture the content of one chamomile sachet, or 10g (0.4oz) of chamomile blossoms and stir gently. Add a few drops of yellow coloring and some lemon essence. Pour the mixture into the molds and let it dry. Take the soap out of the molds and finish off drying the bars on a mesh screen, turning them upside down every so often.

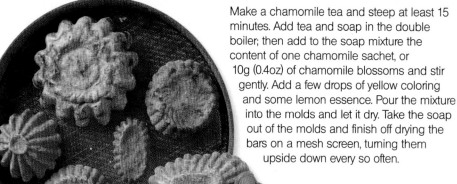

LAVENDER SOAP

- 120g (4.2oz) of vegetable soap flakes
- 90g (3.2oz) of water
- 10g (0.4oz) of dried lavender flowers
- lavender essence
- purple coloring

Especially used to perfume wardrobes and chests of drawers, this soap is also a suitable cosmetic for aging complexions, since it soothes skin irritations and tones up the skin's outermost layers.

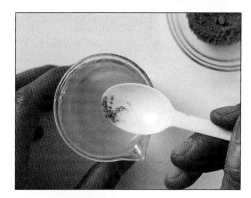
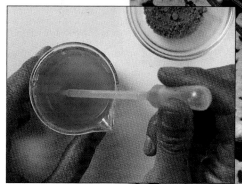

Crumble the dried lavender flowers with a mortar and pestel. Add the soap and scent with a few drops of lavender fragrance. Since tiny lavender flowers may leave stains on white soap, it is best to add some powdered purple coloring, previously melted in warm water. Let the bars of soap dry on a mesh screen, turning them upside down every so often.

ALTHAEA SOAP
(Hollyhock)

You can buy althaea roots either fresh or dried, cut into very small pieces. Either way, it gives soap its strong skin-softening properties.

– 120g (4.2oz) of vegetable soap flakes
– 100g (3.5oz) of water
– 10g (0.4oz) of dried althaea root
– vanilla essence

Prepare an infusion with the dried althaea (hollyhock) root. Boil on a low heat for 15 minutes. Mix it and filter it into a liquid measuring cup, and measure 100g (3.5oz). Melt the soap in the althaea infusion and stir. Althaea root doesn't smell that good, so you may want to add a few drops of vanilla fragrance to scent your soap. Pour into the molds and let it dry thoroughly. Extract your soap from the molds and let it dry out in a well-ventilated place.

SPICY SOAP

A few grams of ginger, nutmeg, cloves or cinnamon are enough to scent and color your soap. The spices' aromas will scent your body every time you bathe and will linger on your skin for the rest of the day.

CINNAMON SOAP

This spice is made from the bark of young branches of the cinnamon tree, dried in the sun until they curl up. Cinnamon bark should be ground in a mortar with a pestel just before use, as it loses most of its lovely scent if crumbled long beforehand.

– 120g (4.2oz) of vegetable soap flakes
– 90g (3.2oz) of water
– 1 tsp. of cinnamon
– cinnamon essence

Melt the soap flakes in water in a double boiler. Add ground cinnamon. Scent with a few drops of cinnamon fragrance, stirring well so it blends in thoroughly. Fill the molds. Cinnamon soap is especially appreciated for its (distinctive) scent but, since it is also very good as a mild skin scrubber, it can be used after a summer vacation, when parched skin needs regenerating after prolonged exposure to the sun.

CLOVE SOAP

Cloves are generally used to flavor food and as ingredients for room sprays. This spice can prevent or cure bacterial infections, but can also cause skin rashes if over-dosed.

– 120g (4.2oz) of
  vegetable soap
  flakes
– 90g (3.2oz) of water
– $1/2$ tsp. of cloves
– clove oil
– ochre coloring

Melt the soap in water in a double boiler and add exactly $1/2$ teaspoon of the ground cloves. Finally, add a few drops of clove oil and a pinch of ochre coloring.

SOFTENING SOAP

This kind of soap is particularly suitable for dry, sensitive skin; thanks to additives such as milk, honey and oils. It makes your skin soft and silky and protects it from the elements.

HONEY SOAP

In winter, when your hands are very dry or chapped, you can soothe them with honey soap. Honey soap is generally suitable for sensitive skin, especially if you are allergic to milk proteins.

- 120g (4.2oz) of vegetable soap flakes
- 90g (3.2oz) of water
- 40g (1.4oz) of honey
- 15g (0.5oz) of sweet almond oil

Melt the soap in water in a double boiler; then add the sweet almond oil and the honey. Gently stir until the mixture has thickened and pour it into the molds.

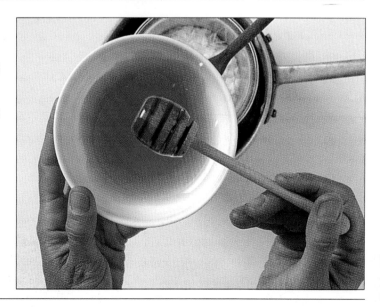

SCRUBBING
SOAP

Thanks to their additives, exfoliating soaps have an energizing effect on your skin, helping it in the process of skin cell regeneration, by removing dead skin. There are many additives to choose from: almond flour, corn flour, bran, wheat germ, among others. Very fine purified sand or ground pumice may also be used.

CORN FLOUR SOAP

From a nutritional point of view, corn is precious for its high content of nitrogenous substances, fats, carbohydrates, mineral salts, vitamin E and vitamin B. Roughly-ground corn flour is an excellent exfoliating agent to use all over your body.

– 120g (4.2oz) of
   vegetable soap flakes
– 90g (3.2oz) of water
– 20-25g (0.7-1oz)
   of roughly-ground
   corn flour

Because of the natural yellow color of corn flour, you do not need to add coloring, but you may like to scent your soap with an essential oil. Melt the soap in a double boiler and add the ground corn flour. Stir the mixture. Pour the mixture into small cake or biscuit molds for pretty and inviting miniature bars of soap.

SOFT WHEAT BRAN SOAP

Soft wheat bran gives soap gentle scrubbing properties (suitable for sensitive skin) as well as lovely hazelnut color streaks.

– 120g (4.2oz) of vegetable soap flakes
– 90g (3.2oz) of water
– 40-50g (1.4-1.8oz) of soft wheat bran

Mix the bran with the soap flakes.
Melt in water and stir until the mixture is completely smooth. Pour it into the molds without leveling the surface too much so that your soap will look slightly rough.

ALMOND FLOUR SOAP

This soap is suitable for both body and face, since almond oil is an excellent skin nourisher.

- 120g (4.2oz) of vegetable soap flakes
- 90g (3.2oz) of water
- 50-70g (1.8-2.5oz) of almond flour
- 1 tsp. of almond oil
- almond essence

After the soap has melted in water and the mixture is smooth, add the almond flour and blend well with the soap.

Add a teaspoon of almond oil and a few drops of almond essence. Let the soap dry thoroughly and store it wrapped in paper to preserve its scent.

WHEAT GERM SOAP

Wheat germ contains plenty of vitamins, mineral salts and micro-nutrients. It nourishes skin cells and prevents moisture loss.

- 120g (4.8oz) of vegetable soap flakes
- 90g (3.6oz) of water
- 15-20g (0.6-0.8oz) of wheat germ flour
- 20g (0.8oz) of honey
- 1 tsp. of wheat germ oil

Add the wheat germ flour to the soap melted in a double boiler, stir well and then add the honey.

Add a teaspoon of oil and stir until the mixture becomes thick. Fill the molds and let it dry.

GLYCERINE "SCULPTURES"

Glycerine is obtained by processing animal and vegetable fats with sodium hydroxide. It can be either added to soap to give it softening properties, or used alone, to create "colored sculptures" that appeal to the eye and caress and pamper your skin.

TRANSPARENT SOAP

You can make soap with glycerine alone. Since this ingredient is rather expensive, use small-size molds.

- *double boiler*
- *block of glycerine*
- *molds*
- *colorings*
- *fragrances*
- *knife*

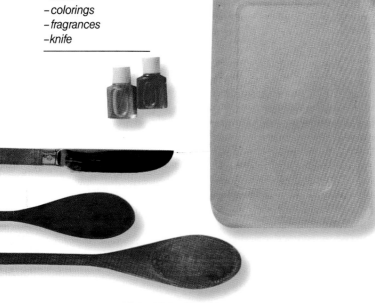

1 – Protect your work table with newspaper or other porous paper. Cut the block of glycerine into small cubes with a sharp knife so it melts faster, and place the cubes in the smaller pot of the double boiler.

2 – Bring the water to a boil in the larger pot. Heat up in a double boiler over a low heat (70°C, 158°F), stirring constantly.

3 – Add a few drops of fragrance and coloring (the less coloring you add, the more transparent your soap will be) and stir well.

4 – Check to make sure there are no air bubbles. If there are, let it rest for five minutes. Pour the liquid glycerine into clean molds.

5 – Cool for about 40 minutes; for faster cooling, put the molds in the freezer.

6 – When the soap is solid, turn the molds upside down on a clean surface.

7 – Let your soap rest for one more hour. Keep it stored in cling wrap to prevent fingerprints and to preserve its scent. After it has become solid, glycerine may be melted again, so if you're not too happy with the result, you can start again.

OPAQUE OR PEARLY GLYCERINE SOAP

- *block of glycerine*
- *colorings*
- *fragrances*
- *talcum powder*

Melt the glycerine in a double boiler. Once it has melted, add in the fragrance and a teaspoon of talcum powder, and stir well. The more opaque and matte-finished you want your soap to be, the more talcum powder you should add.

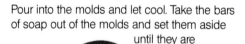

Pour into the molds and let cool. Take the bars of soap out of the molds and set them aside until they are completely dry.

COCOA BUTTER SOAP

Cocoa butter has particular skin clarifying properties. Cocoa butter soap, therefore, is suitable for dry, irritated skin, especially during the harsh winter months.

- *120g (4.2oz) of soap flakes*
- *90g (3.2oz) of water*
- *10g (0.4oz) of cocoa butter*

Slice 10g (0.4oz) of cocoa butter off the block. Melt the cocoa butter in a double boiler, and add the cocoa butter to the melted soap, stirring well until you get an even mixture. Let it cool for a while and fill the molds.

MILK AND HONEY SOAP

This soap is rather soft, has a delicate honey scent, and is particularly suitable for very sensitive skin, such as that of children.

– 120g (4.2oz) of soap flakes
– 90g (3.2oz) of water
– 15-20g (0.5-0.7oz) of dried milk
– 30-40g (1.1-1.4oz) of honey

Melt 15-20g (0.5-0.7oz) of dried milk in 90g (3.2oz) of lukewarm water, getting rid of any lumps. Use this mixture to melt the soap in a double boiler. Add in the honey and stir constantly until the mixture has thickened. Pour into the molds.

"TWO-HALVES" SOAP

If you place the flat sides of two pieces of identical molds over each other, you will be able to make luxuriant bars decorated on both sides.

- block of glycerine
- molds
- colorings
- fragrances
- craft knife

1 – Melt the glycerine in a double boiler and add coloring and fragrances. Pour it into the molds.

2 – Let cool completely and remove from the molds.

3 – Fill the other identical molds with glycerine in the same color and, while it is still hot and liquid, place each one of the ready half bars on top of every mold.

4 – After allowing it to cool, take the soap out of the mold. Remove any glycerine leaks around the junction point of the half bars with a craft knife.

TRANSPARENT SOAP "JAILS"...

The main feature of glycerine is transparency. You can use its clear consistency to make innumerable charming creations by adding different materials to the molds. You can add matte soap cut into geometrical shapes, delicate dried-flower compositions, little shells, precious pearls, or anything else you can imagine.

- *block of glicerine*
- *pieces of soft colored soap*
- *colorings*
- *fragrances*
- *sharp knife*
- *large molds*

1 – Use a sharp knife to cut 5 mm (0.2") thick slices off a bar of rather soft, colored soap. Shape the slices into geometrical figures or hearts, stars, sticks, or whatever you like, and arrange them in a composition on the bottom of the mold.

2 – Melt the glycerine in a double boiler over a low fire and add a few drops of coloring and the fragrance of your choice. Slowly pour the glycerine into a mold, taking care not to alter the arrangement of the pieces of soap you placed on the bottom.

3 – Allow to cool and remove from the mold.

...OF DRIED FLOWERS

To make these exquisite bars of soap you will need different-colored flowers picked in the spring and dried between the pages of a book. When you wash with them, the lovely fragrances trapped in the soap will surely surprise you.

– block of glycerine
– yellow coloring
– flower essences
– a pair of tweezers
– dried flowers
– large molds

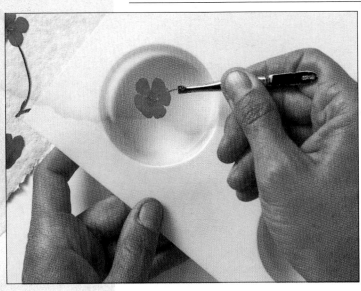

1 – Arrange the dried flowers in a composition on the bottom of the mold.

2 – Cut the glycerine into small pieces and melt it, color it and scent it with a few drops of flower essence.

3 – Gently pour it into the mold, taking care not to alter the arrangement of the flowers placed on the bottom.

4 – Allow the soap to cool and remove it from the mold.

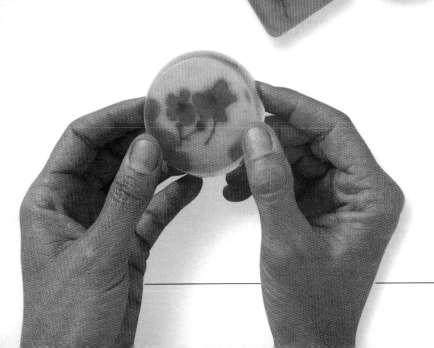

...OF PEARLS

- block of glycerine
- colorings
- fragrances
- synthetic pearls
- shell-shaped molds

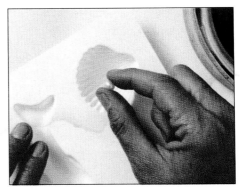

1 – Melt the glycerine in a double boiler. Color it with pale nuances (a few drops of coloring are enough) and add the fragrance.

2 – Choose a shell-shaped mold and place a pearl inside it.

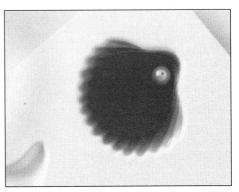

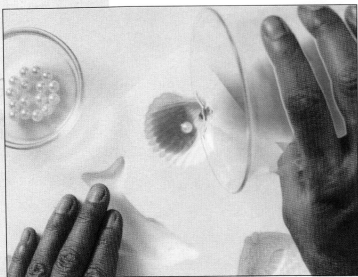

3 – Pour liquid glycerine into the mold and cool without moving. This way, you will have colored "pearl" oysters!

A SOAP CAROUSEL

SHOWER SOAP WITH HANDLES

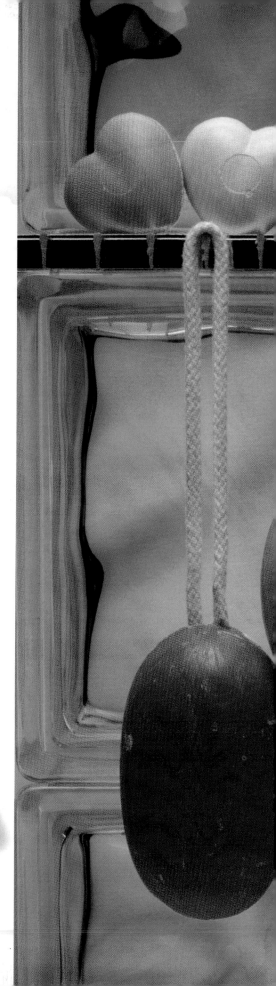

These bars of "soap on a rope" are really easy to make and very handy when you're in the shower. Let your sense of style and creativity guide your choice of shapes, colors and scents.

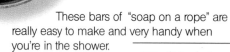

- 120g (4.8oz) of vegetable soap flakes
- 90g (3.6oz) of water
- semi-spherical (or oval) mold, split into two parts
- 50cm (20") of cotton string
- fragrances
- craft knife

1 – Melt the soap in water in a double boiler. Scent it with a few drops of a fragrance of your choice.

2 – Pour it into the first half of a semi-spherical mold. Dig a groove on only this half of the soap for the folded string.

3 – Allow it to cool and remove from the mold.

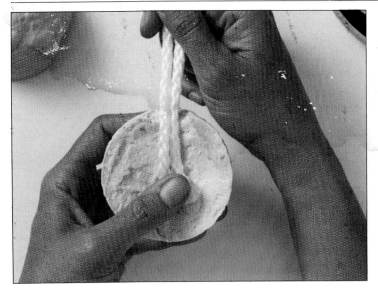

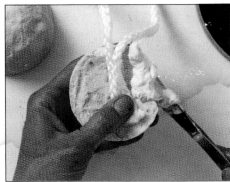

4 – Make the other half of the bar of soap with the same technique. Now fold the string in half. Keeping them parallel, place both ends of the string along the groove of the bar of soap while it is still soft.

5 – Now place the first half of the soap on top of the second one and gently press to make them stick to each other.

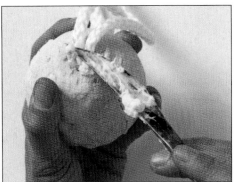

6 – Allow to cool and tightly seal the end where the string is sticking out with a bit of hot soap. Remove any solidified soap drips with a craft knife.

FLOATING SOAP

With these amusing floating bars you won't have to search frantically for soap in the bath tub! Fish and shells floating in the water will also make an enjoyable bath time for your children.

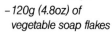

- *120g (4.8oz) of vegetable soap flakes*
- *100g (4oz) of water*
- *fragrances*
- *hand mixer*
- *molds*
- *spoon*

Melt the soap in water in a double boiler and pour it into a glass bowl. Whisk until you get a frothy mousse.
Scent it with a few drops of a fragrance of your choice.
Use a spoon to fill the molds and let the soap liquid cool. Once it dries, you can use this soap while you bathe. The trapped air lowers the soap's density, and the soap will stay afloat.

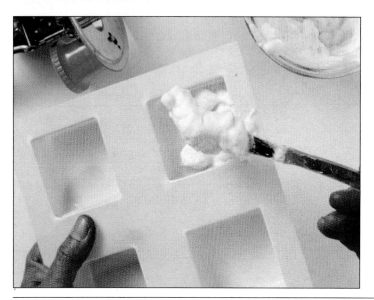

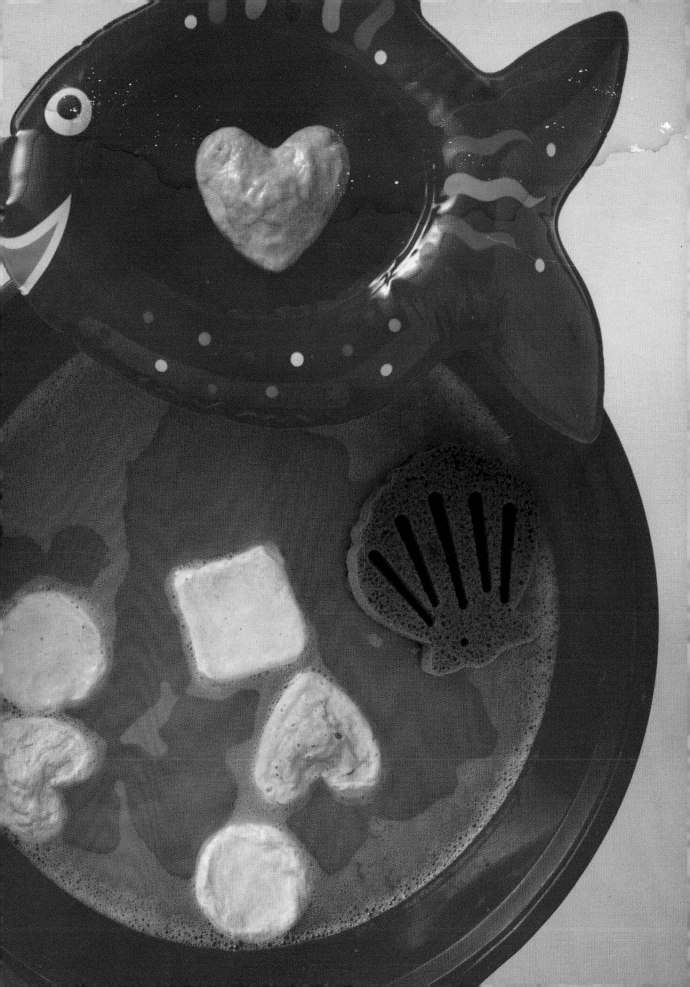

SEMI-TRANSPARENT SOAP

Making this kind of soap is not easy. Even for the more experienced soap maker, it represents quite a challenge. However, if results are not what you expect, you can melt the soap again and start over from scratch. With some practice, you will certainly succeed!

- 120g (4.2oz) of basic soap with a high content of coconut and castor oil
- 90g (3.2oz) of water
- 70g (2.5oz) of rough sugar crystals
- 90g (3.2oz) of 80 proof whiskey

Crumble the soap in a bowl and add the water gradually, stirring with a wooden spoon. Heat the soap in a double boiler over low heat. When the soap has melted completely, add sugar and whiskey. Keep on heating the soap, stirring constantly. When a thin film appears on the surface, remove that film and continue heating the rest of the soap until it looks clear; this allows the alcohol to evaporate and removes any impurities that come to the surface. Every now and then you should test the progress by pouring a little soap into a glass bowl, cooling it and checking whether it is already semi-transparent. Bear in mind that you won't get the same transparency as glycerine soap, but the more impurities you remove, the clearer your soap will be.

SOAP NECKLACES

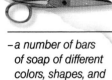

- *a number of bars of soap of different colors, shapes, and scents*
- *a knitting needle*
- *rough string (or natural or colored raffia)*

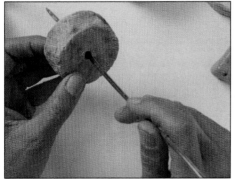

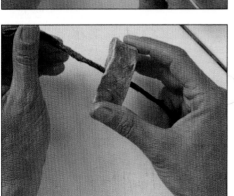

Make a number of bars of soap of different shapes and colors and thread them on a rope with a knitting needle. You can use natural or vegetable-tinted string or some raffia threads with about ten bars of soap, creating unlimited combinations. Make patterns alternating colors and shapes, separating each bar from the next with knots, shells or dried flowers.

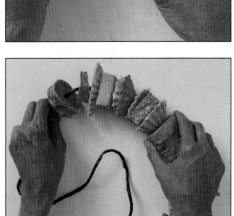

FOAMS AND CRYSTALS

BATH SALTS

Bath salts are fun and beautiful. In fact, they are often bought more for their colors and scents than for their cosmetic properties. To make them yourself, always choose sea salt (either in small or big crystals). Carefully select the essential oils for scenting your salts. Remember that a few drops will be more than enough. A warm bath, in which you have dissolved some bath salts, has a highly refreshing and invigorating power.

- *sea salt*
- *green coloring powder*
- *dwarf pine essence*
- *large bowl*
- *wooden spoon*
- *jar or bottle with top*

1 – Place big crystals of sea salt in a large bowl. Add a few grams of green coloring powder.

2 – Stir with a spoon until all salt crystals have absorbed the color. You may add more coloring if you prefer a brighter hue.

3 – A few drops of dwarf pine will be more than enough to scent your salts and give them balsamic properties.

4 – Store your bath salts in a tightly closed glass jar.

SHAMPOO

An indispensable ingredient in the preparation of liquid shampoo is pectin. This vegetable polysaccharide is used to thicken all ingredients in order to prevent them from separating. Since it is a product also used in the kitchen, you will find it in all food shops or supermarkets.

- *120g (4.2oz) of vegetable soap flakes*
- *730g (26oz) of water*
- *1/2 tsp. of pectin powder*
- *chamomile oil*
- *cinnamon leaf essence*
- *rosemary essence*
- *geranium essence*
- *bottle or jar with top or cork*

2 – Melt the soap in water in a double boiler.

3 – Add a half teaspoon of pectin powder and stir until the mixture looks fluid.

1 – Put in a few drops of chamomile oil, which has soothing qualities on your scalp and is particularly suitable for blond hair. If your hair is dark, replace chamomile oil with rosemary oil, for extra shine.

4 – Add cinnamon oil (a blood circulation booster and a good skin energizer as well) and geranium oil. Stir well. Do not use more than two-four drops of each kind of oil, as too much oil may become irritating to the skin and scalp.

5 – Fill a bottle with your shampoo, close the top and shake well before use.

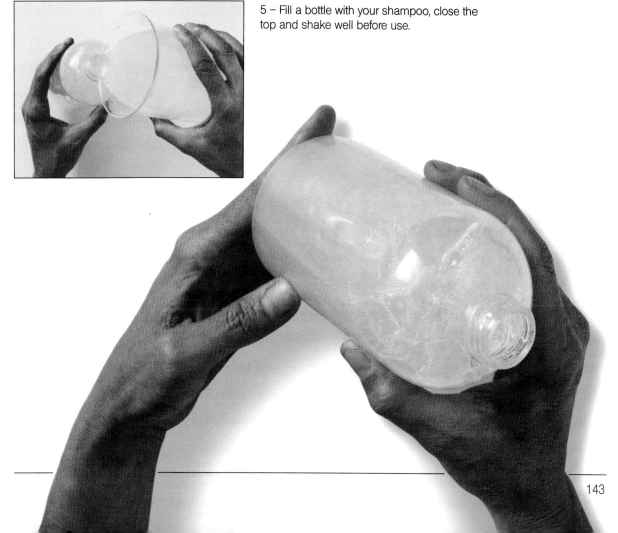

LIQUID SOAP

If you need a bath product with therapeutic properties, follow this recipe. Its ingredients will allow you to make liquid soap with skin-astringent and antibacterial qualities.

- 100g (3.5oz) of vegetable soap flakes
- 420g (14.8oz) of water
- sage oil
- lemon essence
- ground sage
- soap bottle with dispenser

1 – Melt the soap in water in a double boiler, stirring constantly.

2 – Finely cut the sage and add one teaspoon of it to the melted soap.

3 – Add the sage oil (three-six drops).

4 – Add the same amount of lemon fragrance. Stir and check the consistency: if it's not thick enough, add more soap; if it's too thick, add more water.

5 – When the density is right, pour the liquid soap into a dispenser bottle. Shake well before use.

DECORATIONS
AND PACKAGES

A SOAP ALPHABET

- stamps with the
  letters of the
  alphabet
- small bars of soap

Here's how to create a decorative soap
alphabet: stamp the letters into the surface
of the soap after it has been taken out of
the mold and left to dry for one or two hours
but hasn't yet hardened completely. Soft
soap allows you to carve the letters in very
neatly, by gently pressing on the stamps.

LABELS, WHAT A PASSION

First of all, choose the picture or the label you want to use for your soap decoration; make sure its size fits that of your soap so the picture can be placed right in the center of it. Select images whose colors match your soap or, if that's not possible, try to find a picture that calls to mind the ingredients.

- *small labels from magazine or book clippings*
- *scissors*
- *bars of soap*
- *paraffin*
- *brush*

Use a small pair of scissors to cut out the label and trim it all around. In the meantime, melt the paraffin in a double boiler (Caution: Paraffin is highly flammable at high temperatures). Now take a smooth-surfaced bar of soap, brush a little paraffin on the area where the label is supposed to stick, and gently press the label on it. Check that it's perfectly in place and brush it again with paraffin. This way, the label will stay where it is. If you have added too much paraffin and can hardly see the label underneath, remove the excess with a cottonball soaked with olive oil.

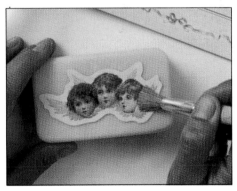

SPRINGTIME HARMONIES

- dried flowers of
  various colors
- scissors
- tweezers
- bars of soap
- paraffin
- brush
- cling wrap or tissue
  paper

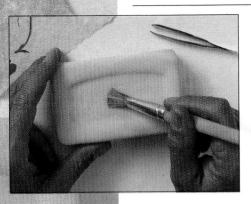

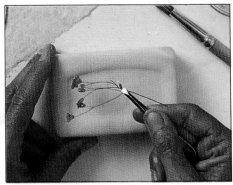

The same technique used with labels or pictures can be applied to dried flowers. Choose the best flowers out of those you picked in the spring and stashed away to dry between the pages of a book, preferably matching the color of your soap. Brush a little paraffin on a smooth area of the bar of soap. Place the dried flowers on it, arranging them neatly and aesthetically; brush again with paraffin. The second brushing requires that the paraffin be very fluid, and therefore very hot. When the paraffin is perfectly dry, wrap your soap with cling wrap or white or colored tissue paper.

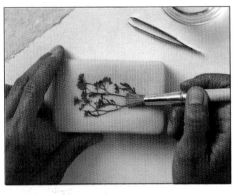

GIFT WRAPS

To scent your wardrobes and chests of drawers, place a few little bars of soap in linen, cotton, or lace sachets. The soap will slowly give off its scent through the fibers of the fabric.

When your soap has dried completely you can start thinking of pretty gift wraps, so there is no need to hurry. In the meantime keep it stored in little cardboard boxes and leave it to dry in a warm, airy place for as long as needed. Scented soap is usually wrapped to prevent its essential oils from evaporating, so wrap it in cling wrap first and deal with the gift wrap later.

You can use colored paper, ribbons, corrugated cardboard, raffia or string, balsa wood boxes, precious trimming, lace, or bunches of dried flowers. As a final touch, write and attach a little reminder card with the ingredients and the properties of your homemade soap.

LACE AND...

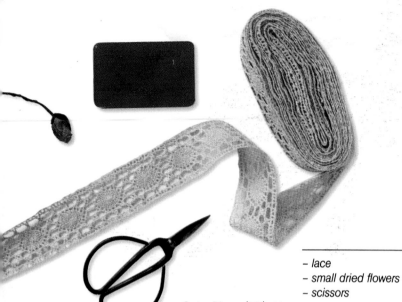

- lace
- small dried flowers
- scissors

Cut a 50-cm (20") strip of handmade écru lace and iron it with care. Wrap the soap in it, keeping the lace very tight around it. Tie the ends and insert a small dried flower of a matching color. You can see other suggestions on the photograph on the next page.

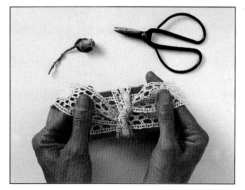